The Cadence of
WAR

by Nicholas DeLibero • illustrated by Ovi Hondru

Table of Contents

Chapter 1

May 18, 1864

"Ma, please?" Billy begged. "I am fifteen years old now, and Pop and Mr. Sanders already left for war. Even Jimmy Sanders went to enlist, and he's a year younger than me. It is important that all able-bodied men in Ohio join up. I need to help. It would make Pop proud."

Amanda Guild looked at her son sadly.

"Billy, I cannot bear sending you off to war. The thought of someone at the door holding an envelope . . ." Mrs. Guild trailed off as she looked out the window. "I already said good-bye to your father last month when he left. I need you safe at home to help with your sisters and brother. Please give up this nonsense, I beg you."

Billy pictured his mother receiving a letter about his death and cringed, but he felt more angry than afraid. He stormed out into the farm and slammed the door behind him, sprinting toward his favorite buckeye tree, under which he always sat when he wanted **serenity**. Billy's solace was cut short when his younger brother Toby jogged toward the tree.

"Mommy is crying," Toby blurted out. The last thing Billy wanted to do was reason with a six-year-old.

"It's not fair," he muttered to Toby as he picked up a rock and threw it in disgust. "I want to go to war and fight. You're too little to understand."

"Will you see Daddy?" asked Toby.

"I'll do whatever it takes," said Billy and pointed to the house. "Now go back inside to Ma."

Billy leaped up and headed to town. *I need to find a way to help my country in this war*, he thought.

"Is anyone home? It's Billy Guild," yelled Billy as he knocked on a large white door. As the door creaked open, a stern-faced woman with brown hair and green eyes poked her head out. Mrs. Morris was regarded as the nastiest woman in town. Ever since he accidently broke her front gate last spring, Billy always felt intimidated by her.

"Is Ben home?" he asked while avoiding eye contact. Mrs. Morris grunted and said, "Out back, doing chores." Billy nodded a quick "thank-you" and ran around to the backyard, where his best friend was chopping wood.

"I'm going to the recruitment office," Billy told Ben

breathlessly. "I'm going into town to sign up for the war! I don't think I want to go alone, though. What do you say about joining me?"

Ben dropped his armful of wood and grabbed Billy by the shoulders. "Anything to get away from my mom," he replied.

The two left Ben's house and walked to town. Though Billy was excited at first, he became extremely anxious.

"So how are we going to lie about our age?" Ben asked. The legal age to sign up for war was eighteen. If the boys revealed their real age, they would immediately be denied.

"Keep a straight face and say, 'I look young for my age,'" Billy instructed.

When they reached the recruitment office, a large crowd of men greeted them. Posters were plastered all over the building, enticing people to join the war effort. Inside, a pudgy man in uniform sat behind a small wooden table.

"Next," he called, and Billy crept to the table. Now that he was about to sign up, his heart melted in his chest. He was not expecting a crowd this large to be watching.

"Sir, I—I—I'd like to sign up to be a soldier," Billy stammered. Billy didn't realize that the recruiting officer was the town butcher, Mr. Herald.

The man said, "Name?"

"Billy Guild, sir."

"Are you Charlie's boy?" asked Mr. Herald.

Billy felt a short burst of **reassurance**. Maybe he had a way in. "Yes, I am," he responded.

"And how old are you, Billy?"

"I'm eighteen, sir," Billy said, as his eyes lowered to the man's desk.

"I ran into your mother last Friday," explained Mr. Herald, his brow furrowed. "She said she was buying chicken for your fifteenth birthday dinner."

Billy's visions of heroism vanished.

"I should dismiss you for lying," said Mr. Herald. "However, I have two spots open for drummer boys. You want to do your part?"

Billy imagined his mother and family fighting their own war, one that existed on the home front. He wouldn't be able to lend a hand to his family when they needed it most, but this was his chance to not only make his father proud but to serve his country.

"We'll put you with the 168th **Regiment** Ohio Volunteer Infantry," said Mr. Herald. "Your father is enlisted there, but don't expect to run into him. He's with the first group of soldiers and probably miles away from the camp where you're going to train. Sign here and you'll be all set. And, son," the man glanced up, "good luck to you."

"Um . . . thank you, sir," Billy answered.

Billy walked away as Mr. Herald called for the next person and Ben shuffled past him for his chance to sign up.

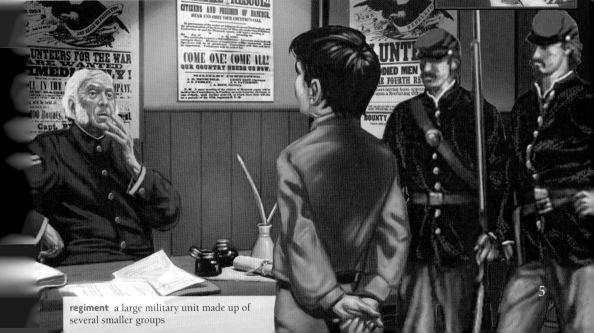

regiment a large military unit made up of several smaller groups

5

It was late in the afternoon when Billy finally returned home. His mother was working in the garden pulling out dead buckeye roots.

"I didn't want to tell you like this, but what's done is done," stated Billy. "I enlisted today."

Shocked by her son's words, Mrs. Guild dropped her gardening tools. "How could they take you? You are only fifteen."

"I am officially a drummer boy. Ben and I signed up today. If I can't be a solider, I can at least help the cause."

"I just ask that you come home to me, Billy," his mother said quietly. She stumbled back into the house toward her other children and wept, as their small arms wrapped tightly around her waist.

Chapter 2

June 6, 1864

The battle hadn't started, yet Billy already felt the **repercussions** of war. It was the beginning of June, and summer's **grueling** heat was on the brink. The six-mile trek to Camp Dennison at 6:00 A.M. was an exhausting exercise in physical and mental endurance. Ben hustled behind Billy, gasping for air every thirty seconds.

The camp would serve as a training center for the men before they were transferred to Cynthiana, Kentucky. Instead of resembling a powerful man, Billy felt like a pitiful child. Marching along with the 168th Regiment, Billy thought *this is a soldier's war, not a place for drummer boys.*

A towering shadow suddenly lurked over the boys, wearing full Union army **regalia**. The man walked by Billy and started screaming at a soldier. Mrs. Morris was no longer the most intimidating person Billy had ever met!

"Do you not know the difference between your left and right foot?" screamed the man. The soldiers were to march in unison, but the journey made them tired. "Let me remind you," continued the man as he took his gun and struck the soldier on the left foot. "This is your left; you lead with *it!*"

7

Although Billy would normally feel too nervous to address a soldier, he tapped the man in front of him on the back.

"Excuse me, sir, but who is that army sergeant?"

"That is no sergeant," answered the soldier. "That is Colonel Conrad Garis. He's in charge of the whole regiment."

As the regiment made its way to Camp Dennison, the Ohio River began to emerge. Billy wanted to dive headfirst into the river and cool off, but first he needed to set up camp.

"Here's your new home, boys," said a lieutenant when the regiment arrived at the campgrounds. "Don't expect to find your momma here," he laughed annoyingly. "You can kiss her wholesome cooking good-bye."

The new arrivals were then instructed to set up their tents. To conserve space, the army required twenty men to occupy one tent, even though a tent fit only twelve men comfortably. Billy and Ben were ordered to share a tent with the soldiers who were under the age of twenty-one.

The boys dropped their bags and helped construct the tent.

"I know we're close friends," shared Ben, "but I'm not comfortable being *this* close."

Billy thought he heard a gun blast and jumped in the air. He then realized with embarrassment that it was only the sound of his stomach rumbling. It was now late in the day, and the hike had made him extremely hungry.

"I wish this **hardtack** was roast chicken instead of a moldy biscuit," complained Billy. He tried to break off a piece, but the food was solid as a rock. Another young soldier noticed Billy's frustration.

"You shouldn't waste all of your rations right away," said nineteen-year-old Chris Gabel. "That hardtack may taste awful, but it will save you from depleting your meat rations."

Each soldier was provided with twenty ounces of salt and fresh beef, a pound of flour, and whatever vegetable was on hand prior to leaving camp. The regiment was equipped with food for now, but it was never certain when the supply trains would reach them.

"Are we the only group of soldiers here?" Billy asked Chris.

"As far as I know, yes. I think the first group took off for Cynthiana last week."

Billy's nerves writhed through his skin. There was a chance his father was already involved in combat.

hardtack a hard biscuit made from flour and water; the word tack comes from the British slang for food

Chapter 3

June 9, 1864

Rat-a-tat—tat-tat-tat.

Lieutenant Ragan's drum boomed, and Billy and Ben worked hard to replicate its **cadence**. The boys had been practicing since 7:00 A.M., and Billy's fingers were starting to blister. It was important for them to learn the exact drum beats officers depended on them to produce in battle to signal the troops. There were fifteen drumbeats, but the most important to learn were for signaling when to attack, stop, retreat, and move forward. Lieutenant Ragan was in charge of instructing the boys.

"Here's how you grip the sticks," explained the muscular, full-bearded officer. "There is the traditional grip and the match grip. The traditional is more difficult to master."

Rat-a-tat—tat-tat-tat.

"Since the noise level of battle is so loud," continued Lieutenant Ragan, "the drumbeats are used to replace shouting out commands."

"I'll never get this," said Ben.

"Sure you will," Billy assured him. "Listen." Billy played the cadence again and again for his friend. After the three-hour practice session, Ben was ready to throw his sticks into the Ohio River.

"You can do it. Keep trying," encouraged Billy.

Rat-a-tat—tat-tat-tat.

"Wait . . . I think I'm starting to get it!" Ben said joyfully.

The boys looked at each other eagerly, but Ben's expression soon transformed into a look of concern.

Lieutenant Ragan proceeded to show the boys how to fix the drum strap in case it snapped off of their shoulders.

"Take this," Lieutenant Ragan said as he tossed two rags at the boys. "Just in case the drum head gets dirty. And if we make it through the first drill," he added, "I'll show you how to change the drum head properly."

Ben took a slow breath and attempted to play the beat once more.

"What does this rhythm mean again?" he asked.

"It means that the **Rebels** are coming and the troops need to assemble, with **muskets** ready," said Billy.

"Oh, that's right—" Ben sighed, looking discouraged. "It's so hard to keep all these signals straight."

Remembering all of the beats came easily to Billy. As the drills progressed, he began to feel a sense of confidence about his role as a drummer boy.

* * *

Rebels a term for Confederate soldiers, used mainly by Northerners
muskets large firearms commonly used by soldiers of the period

Later that evening, Billy and Ben sat around the campfire with some of the soldiers. Billy sat close to the fire, stretching out his sore and tired hands over the flames. For Billy, it felt strange to be sitting with the older men, but the soldiers seemed to enjoy having the boys around.

"Hey, fellows, what'd you learn today?" One of the men elbowed Billy in the ribs and winked toward Ben, "*Rat-a-tat, rat-a-tat*? Doesn't that mean it's time to eat?"

"Yeah," another soldier called out jokingly. "You're doing all the fun work while we're exiled to the fields to run drills."

Billy felt an arm hanging loosely around his shoulder.

"You know, you remind me a lot of my son. You're both roughly the same age, and you both are tall. The only

difference is that my boy has blond hair instead of jet-black. I'm Jason Conley."

He then tossed Billy a small bag.

"I bought these from a sutler this afternoon. My boy would be upset if he knew that I didn't share these with you."

Inside the bag were three meat pies and a deck of cards. "Go back to your tent and play a game of cards. Get some rest."

Billy felt guilty for taking the bag. Sutlers sold products at steep prices to desperate soldiers. Jason had probably paid a hefty amount of money for the goods.

"Thanks! I love meat pies," Billy said. "But I can't take them. Well, maybe one." Jason's generosity reminded Billy of his father. He couldn't help but smile.

15

sutler a civilian merchant who sells goods to an army in the field

Chapter 4

June 10, 1864

Early the next morning, the ignited attitudes of camp were extinguished like a flame when the boys were awakened by the officers. It was time to report to Harrison County in Kentucky, where the battle of Cynthiana was taking place. It would be a twenty-three-hour journey on foot without stopping.

"Come, boys, quickly," Lieutenant Ragan shouted. "Billy, you come with me. And Ben, you head out with Gabel. The Rebels have been spotted and we must prepare for battle."

Billy and Ben jumped up and grabbed their drums. They were divided up, with Billy leading one section of the regiment and Ben leading the other.

"I know we'll see each other again," Billy said as he shook his best friend's hand. Then they picked up their gear and rushed over to the officers they were assigned to.

"Sir, how long until we battle?" Billy asked.

"Soon, Billy. Stick close to me now and listen carefully to my orders," said Lieutenant Ragan. "I'll need you to signal carefully and accurately once battle starts."

"Yes, sir," Billy answered.

There was a full day of marching ahead and Billy knew he must concentrate hard.

"We are going to need more than your drumming skills now, you know," continued Lieutenant Ragan. "You'll have to carry messages across the battlefields, carry stretchers, search for wounded soldiers, and retrieve weapons from the battlefield to be reissued."

The reality of war finally hit Billy. He had not been aware of all the physically demanding and **grotesque** jobs drummer boys were expected to perform. Billy kept thinking about all the times he explained to his mother how strong he was. Now his strength would be tested by carrying the wounded and dead bodies of soldiers.

"Well don't just stand there son," shouted Lieutenant Ragan. "Grab your drum and get moving!"

By the seventeenth hour of marching, Billy had lost
all feeling in his arms. The sweat on his palms made it
impossible to maintain a firm grip of the sticks. The drum
that once seemed so light now weighed on his chest like
a massive tree trunk. He wondered if any of the
soldiers were still actually listening to the drumbeat.
The sound was now deafening to him.

Lieutenant Ragan approached Billy.

"Another six hours to go," the officer reported.
"How's our army's strongest soldier doing?"

Billy's feet hurt, his stomach **convulsed**, and his
head throbbed. He knew to keep his mouth shut and
not to complain to an officer.

"Just doing my duty, sir," he answered while
straightening his posture.

"Well then, continue leading the way."

Billy thought about Ben and wondered if he was struggling. Ben and the second section were a good twenty miles behind. Through all the **anguish**, he couldn't help but laugh to himself. Ben was probably thrilled about playing the simple "march" drumbeat for twenty-three hours. He wouldn't have to worry about mixing up commands.

The lieutenant must have seen Billy smile, for he asked, "What keeps you so motivated, son?"

Billy took his eyes off the drum and looked directly at the officer. "In six hours, I'll be closer to my father."

Upon entering Cynthiana, they found that the town had been **pillaged**. The Rebels had set fire to the streets, destroying half of the storefronts and buildings.

A middle-aged officer approached Lieutenant Ragan. "We've just received word that General Morgan invaded the town this morning and pushed the Union troops toward the northern railroad line," he announced. "We'll need to infiltrate the railroad and attack."

"Billy, order the men to move forward," yelled Lieutenant Ragan.

Billy did a quick drum roll, signaling the regiment to march onward. It was time to engage in war.

Billy directed the regiment to the edge of town, where the railroad tracks began.

Once the regiment reached the foot of the tracks, Colonel Garis assembled the men.

"Our country was founded on the principles of liberty and equality for all men," hollered the colonel as he pointed his bayonet to the sky and clenched his fist. "Our hearts flare with aggression. We will preserve the North!

A young soldier waved a Union flag, further inspiring the regiment.

"These grounds are already consumed with the dead," said Colonel Garis fiercely. "The bodies of our families, friends, and proud Union soldiers fill the fields. Our lives and this country are precious. We will not die for nothing. We fight for the Union. ATTACK!"

Billy beat his drum and signaled the men to charge forward.

Rat-a-tat—tat-tat-tat.

The soldiers quickly dispersed into the fields by the tracks, leaving Billy by himself.

He roamed around the eastern part of the tracks and searched for any wounded soldiers from the prior battle.

Near a tiny stream was an overturned railroad car. It appeared that a soldier had used it as protection from gunfire. Billy approached the wreckage tentatively and removed a giant log that was blocking the entrance of the car. As he lifted the log, he spotted the leg of a soldier sticking out.

"Help! This soldier is trapped!" yelled Billy, his cheeks flushed—but it was too late; the soldier was dead from several bullet wounds.

"NO!" he screamed, now seeing the soldier's face.

It was his schoolteacher, John Sanders. His blood was already dry, confirming the fact that his wounds were not fresh.

Billy collapsed to the ground. For a few minutes, he sat next to his beloved teacher, wondering how he had felt in his last moments of life.

"You did not die in vain," Billy said, and touched the side of Mr. Sanders's cheek.

Before he walked away, Billy searched Mr. Sanders's pockets. He pulled out a photograph of Mrs. Sanders and a packet of letters, bloodstained but still wrapped tightly in twine. He tucked them into his own pocket.

"I promise I will bring these letters back to your wife."

He left the body and turned toward a steep hill. Billy could see that there were many wounded and dead soldiers ahead. The young and old faces haunted Billy's thoughts. As he began to hike up the hill, an audible moan caught his attention. He twisted his head to the left and saw someone moving.

Rushing over to where he had heard the sound, he found a wounded soldier. Covered with dirt and blood, the soldier's face was obscured.

"I will sound for a medic," Billy assured him.

"Bi—Bill—" the raspy voice slowly evaporated as the soldier fell into unconsciousness.

Startled, Billy grabbed his drum rag and wiped the soldier's face.

"Father!" he cried. Billy drummed as loudly as he could. "Is anyone near? I need help!"

A figure approached from the distance. Perhaps Ben had finally made it to the battlefield and could help.

"We're over here. Hurry!" cried Billy.

As the figure came closer, Billy saw a musket being raised. This was no drummer boy but a Rebel soldier. The musket exploded as Billy hurled his body over his father's. The musket ball flew right at him. Billy's fate appeared equal to his father's, as he fainted into a dark oblivion.

Chapter 5

June 12, 1864

"Answer me, son."

The voice echoed through Billy's ears, and his groggy consciousness gave way to an aching head.

"Billy, please wake up."

Billy's right eye started twitching as he slowly tried to open his eyes.

"Uh," grunted Billy in pain. "My head."

"He's awake! Medic!" the man's voice cried out.

That voice had appeared in several of Billy's recent dreams—but everything now felt like a nightmare. His body lay **stagnant** on a table. He figured his brain was damaged, too, because he imagined his father to be very near him.

"Father?" his voice whispered hoarsely. "Are you real?"

"You can hear me!" exclaimed the man lying on the adjacent table as he extended his arm toward the wounded boy. The sound of the familiar voice sent a warm surge through Billy's body. His eyes blinked and his vision started to clear. It was indeed his father, Charlie Guild.

"How did you end up in Cynthiana?" he asked.

It took thirty seconds for Billy to assemble the words, his thoughts still hazy.

"I just wanted . . . to make everyone proud," Billy responded.

Charlie's eyes filled with tears, and the two reached for each other's hands.

"The medic explained to me how you are the drummer boy," said Charlie. "You saved my life, son."

"What happened to me?"

"You used your body to protect mine," explained Charlie. "A Rebel shot at you, hitting your shoulder, but one of our men shot back and he fled. Then your friend Ben Morris found us! I thought I was dreaming when I saw his face. And let me tell you, that boy is strong! He and another soldier carried us to this medical tent."

"Ben arrived?" Billy asked softly.

Charlie still had so many questions for his son, but he knew Billy was in a fragile state.

"Pop, Mr. Sanders is dead," Billy said, a tear falling from the corner of his eye. After a moment, he said with sudden determination, "We can make up for it!"

"No, son. The war is over for us," Charlie said in a soothing voice. "When we both have regained our strength, it'll be time to head home together to our family."

"What about the regiment?" Billy tried to pick himself up from the table, but his arms were lead pipes.

"Another regiment traveled by train and came to our aid. The 171st Ohio National Guard. They pushed the Rebel troops back and forced General Morgan to flee."

"I wanted to serve the Union more, Pop. Being a drummer boy was the closest I could come to being a soldier, and I'd only just begun."

"You *are* a soldier, son," said Charlie. "You don't need the regalia to prove it. You have made it possible for me to return to your mother, and your brother and sisters."

With his father at his side, Billy drifted back to sleep—and dreamed of going back home.

Glossary

anguish   (AN-gwish) *noun* an extreme amount of pain (page 19)

cadence   (KAY-dens) *noun* a regular beat or rhythm; a recurrent sequence of sounds (page 11)

convulsed   (kin-VULSD) *verb* shook uncontrollably (page 18)

grotesque   (groh-TESK) *adjective* unusually strange or disturbing (page 17)

grueling   (GROO-ling) *adjective* exhausting; tiring (page 7)

pillaged   (PIH-lijd) *verb* invaded with violence for the purpose of stealing possessions (page 20)

reassurance   (ree-uh-SHER-uns) *noun* sense of confidence (page 4)

regalia   (rih-GAL-yuh) *noun* various emblems and badges that indicate membership (page 7)

repercussions   (ree-per-KUH-shunz) *noun* unexpected effects of an action or event; often lasting a long time (page 7)

serenity   (suh-REH-nih-tee) *noun* state of peacefulness or calm (page 2)

stagnant   (STAG-nunt) *adjective* inactive; not moving (page 26)

Analyze the Text

Questions for Close Reading

Use facts and details from the text to support your answers to the following questions.

- Why did Billy feel conflicted about joining the Union army? Reference specific text from the story.

- Describe the living conditions of soldiers in a Civil War camp. Quote specific details from the text in your description.

- How do Billy's feelings about being a drummer boy change from the beginning of Chapter 2 to the end of the Chapter 3?

- In Chapter 5, why is Billy upset that he has to return home? What does this tell you about his character?

Comprehension: Analyze Story Elements

This story takes place in three places: Billy's hometown, the training camp, and the battlefield. How does each setting affect the events and Billy's character? Use the chart to identify each location, what happens there, and how it affects Billy's character.

Setting	Events	Character

Little Cat Goes Fast

by Carol Pugliano-Martin • illustrated by John Bennett

Little Cat wants to go fast.

Little Cat rides with her mom.
"Is this fast?" says Mom.
"Too slow!" says Little Cat.

4

Little Cat rides with her dad.
"Is this fast?" says Dad.
"Too slow!" says Little Cat.

7

"Is this ride fast?"
Mom and Dad say.
"Too slow!" says Little Cat.

9

Little Cat wants to go
on this ride.

Up, up, up they go.

13

Down, down, down they go!

Little Cat likes this ride!
Mom and Dad say,
"Too fast!"